The AMAZING 50 STATES

MAZE BOOK

By Scott Sullivan

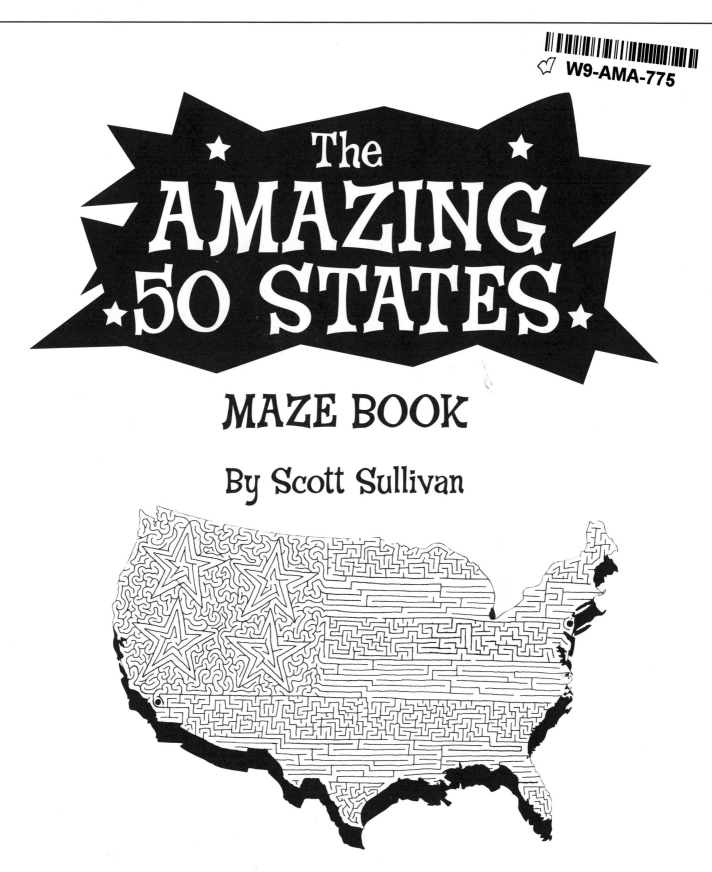

Take a trip through the U.S., traveling from a state's capital to one of its major cities.

PRICE STERN SLOAN

Copyright © 2001 by Scott Sullivan. All rights reserved. Published by Price Stern Sloan,
a division of Penguin Young Readers Group, 345 Hudson Street, New York, New York 10014.
PSS! is a trademark of Penguin Group (USA) Inc. Published simultaneously in Canada. Printed in the U.S.A.

Some of this material appeared previously in Tough Mazes II States of Confusion Maze Funbook, copyright © 1990 Scott Sullivan.

ISBN 978-0-8431-7656-8

Alabama

Alaska

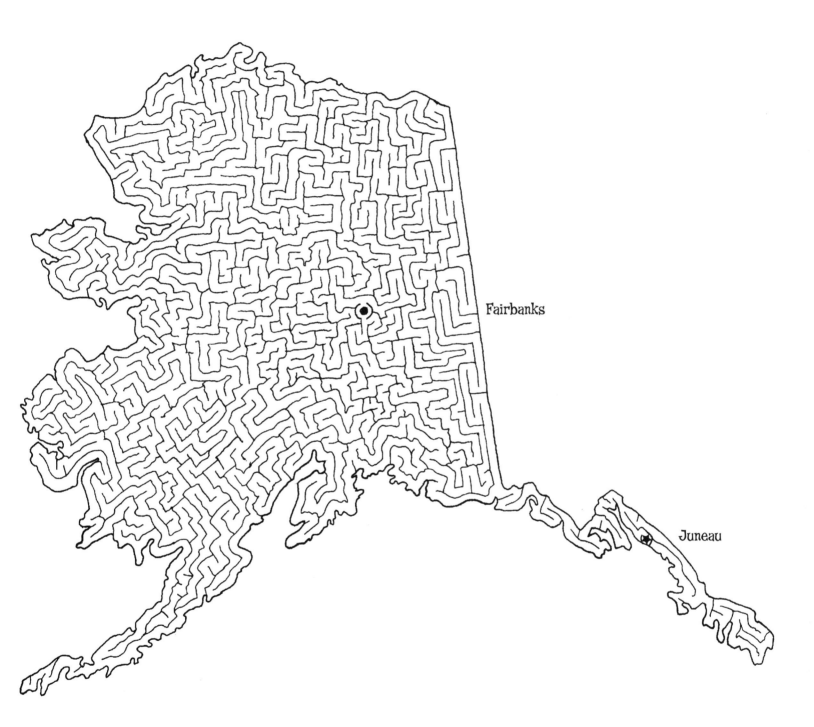

Arizona

Flagstaff

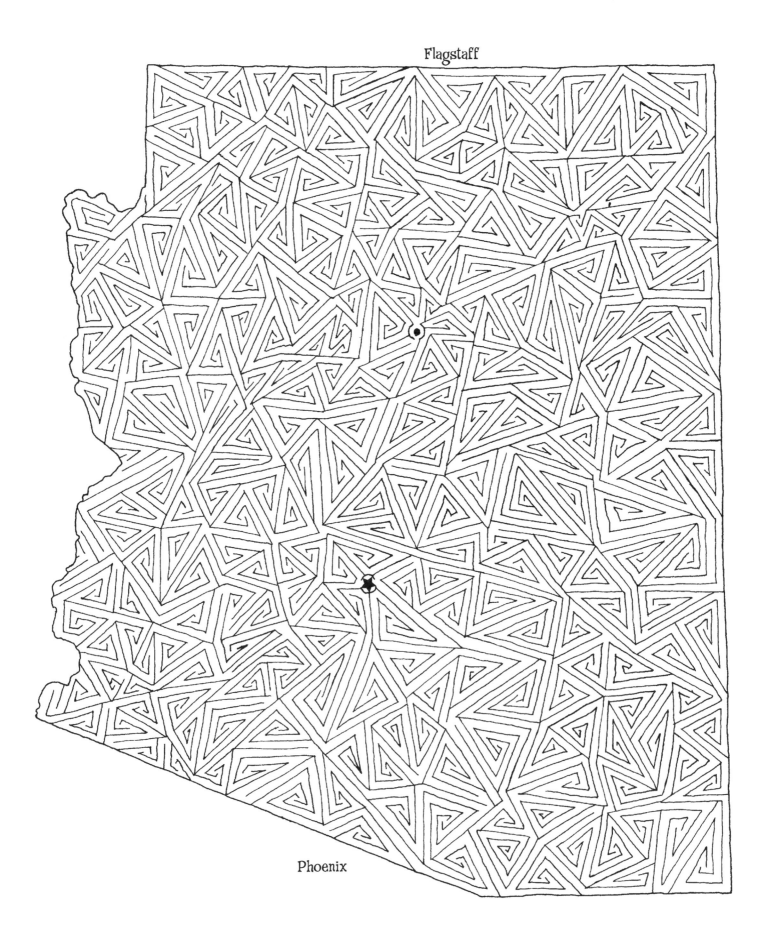

Phoenix

Arkansas

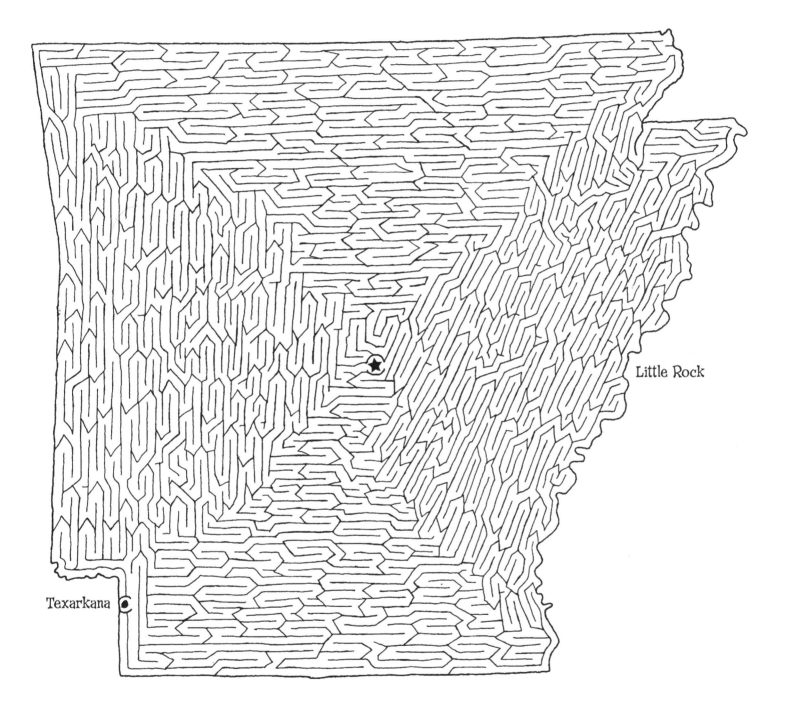

Little Rock

Texarkana

California

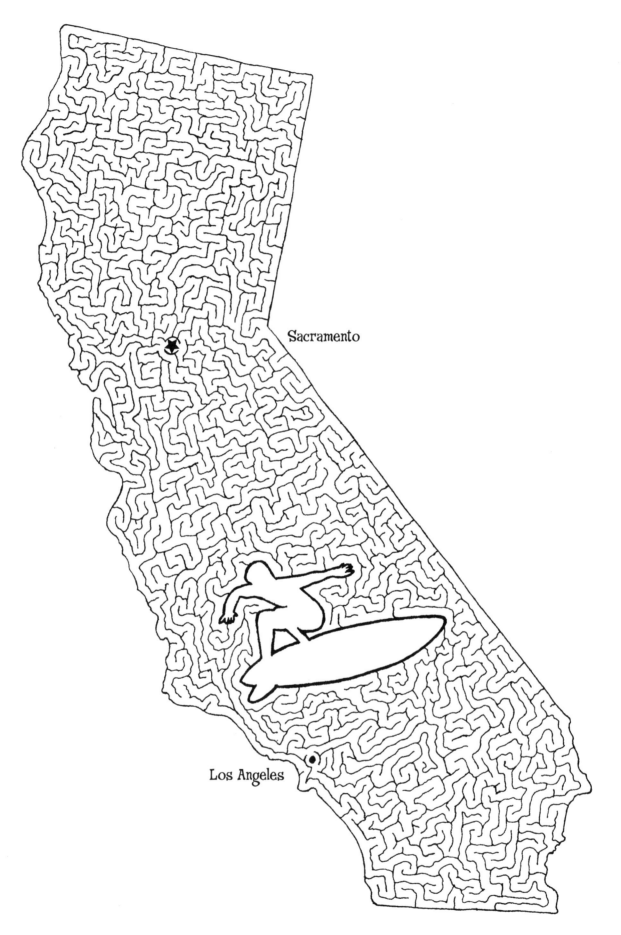

Sacramento

Los Angeles

Colorado

Denver

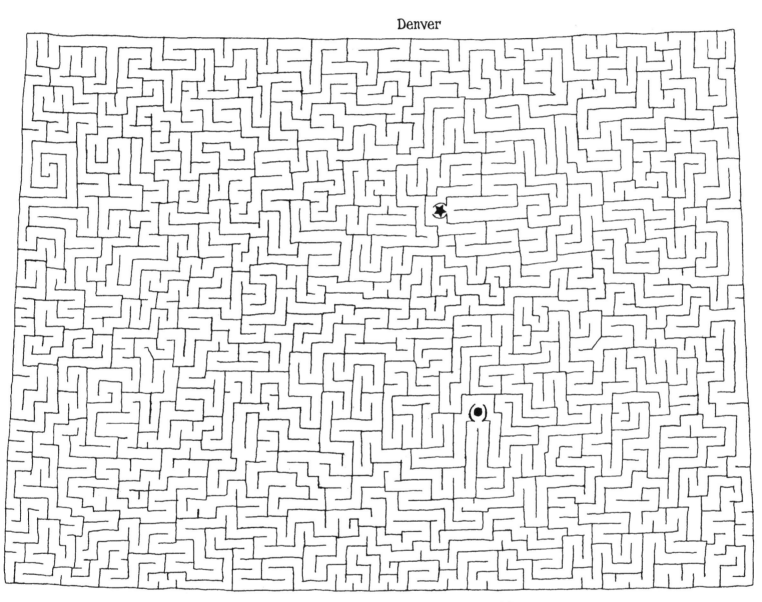

Pueblo

Connecticut

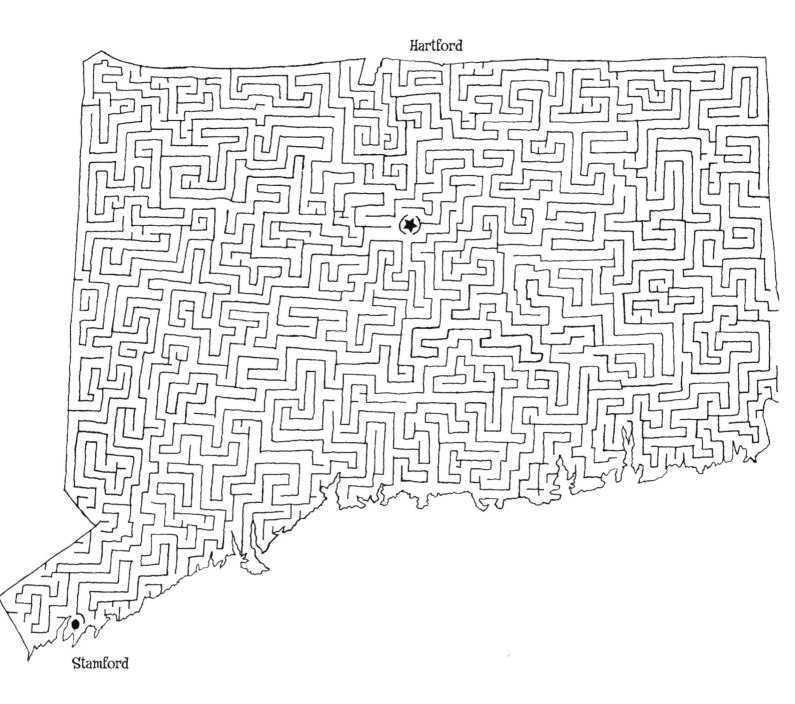

Hartford

Stamford

Delaware

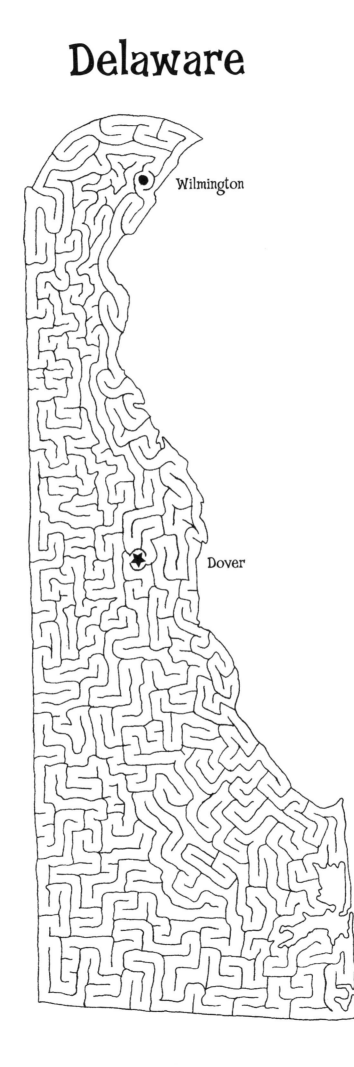

Wilmington

Dover

Florida

Tallahassee

Miami

Georgia

Atlanta

Macon

Hawaii

Honolulu

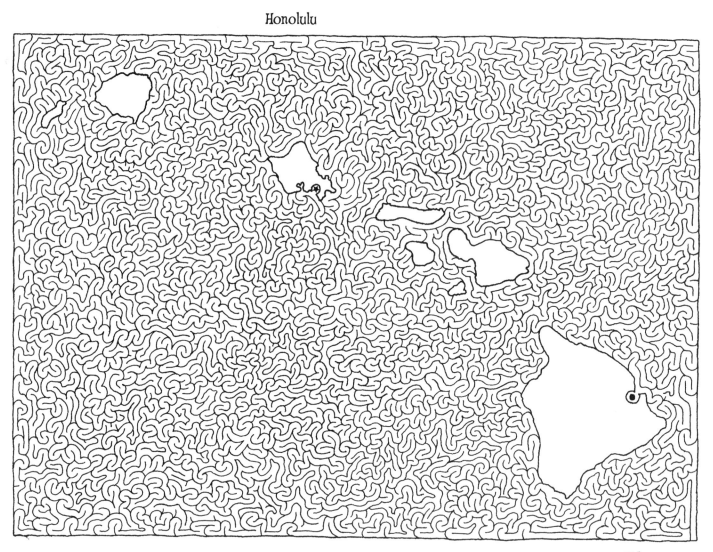

Hilo

Idaho

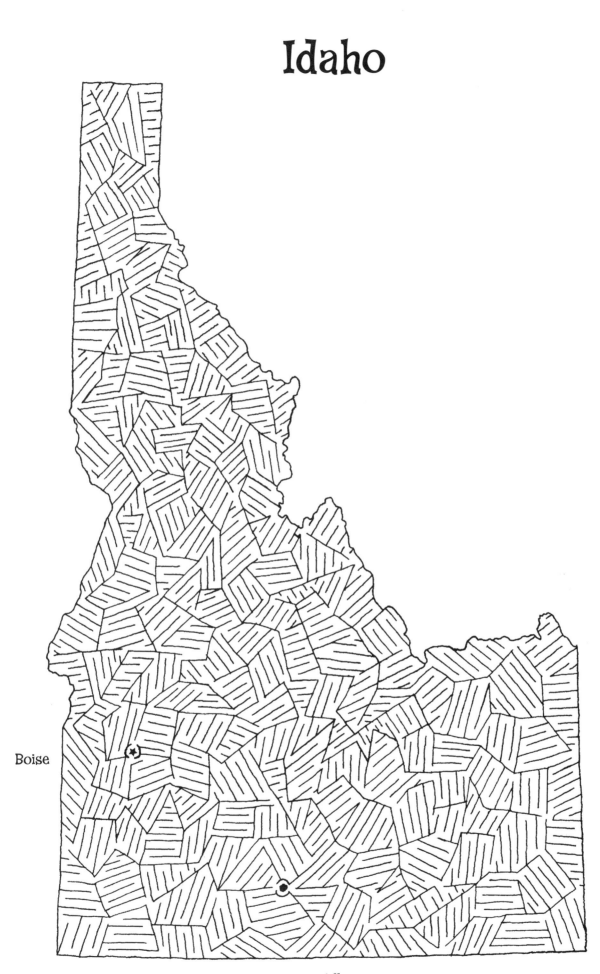

Boise

Twin Falls

Illinois

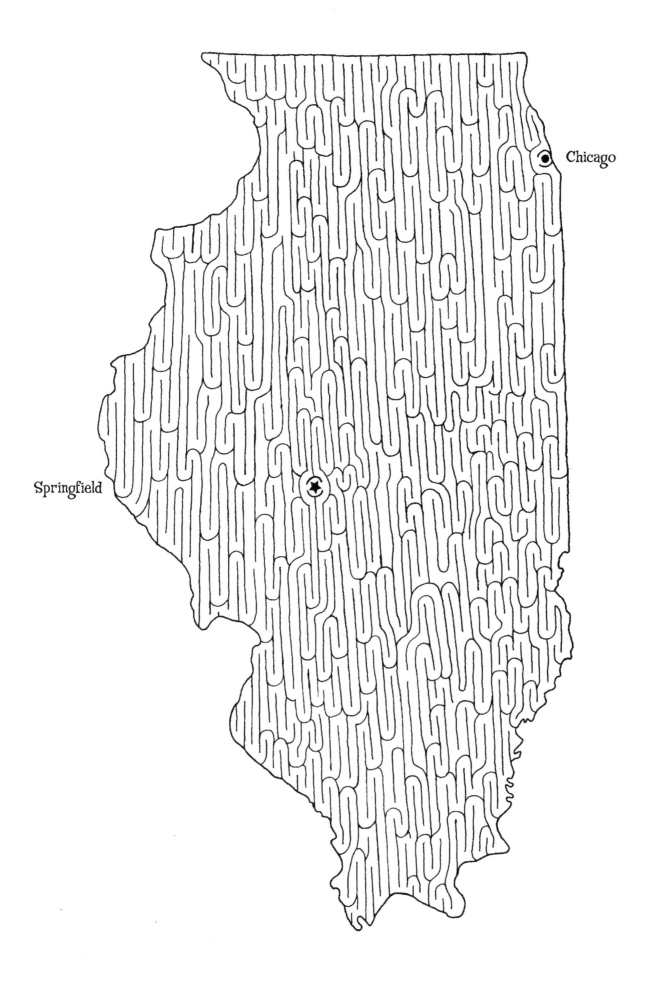

Chicago

Springfield

Indiana

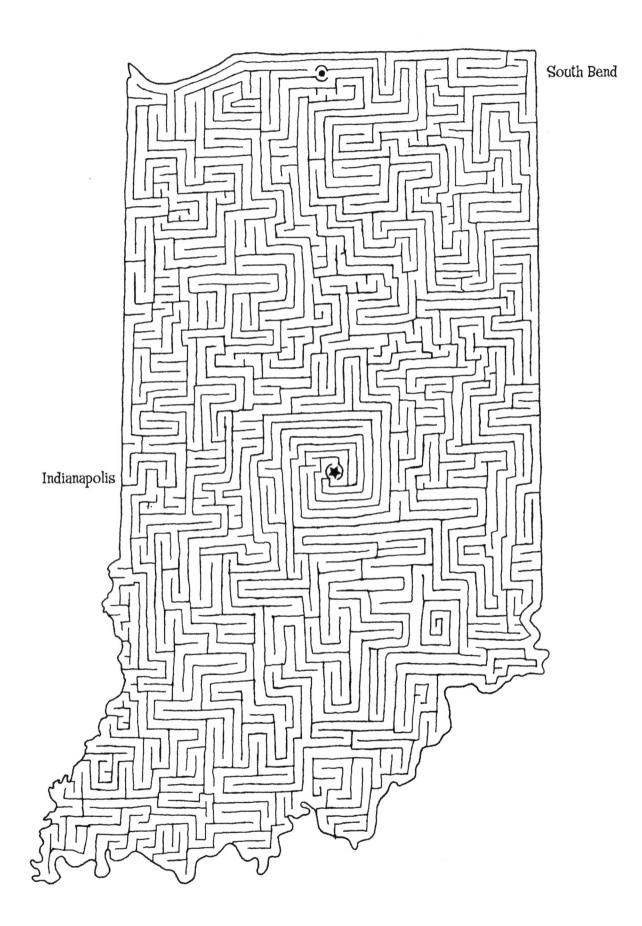

South Bend

Indianapolis

Iowa

Cedar Rapids

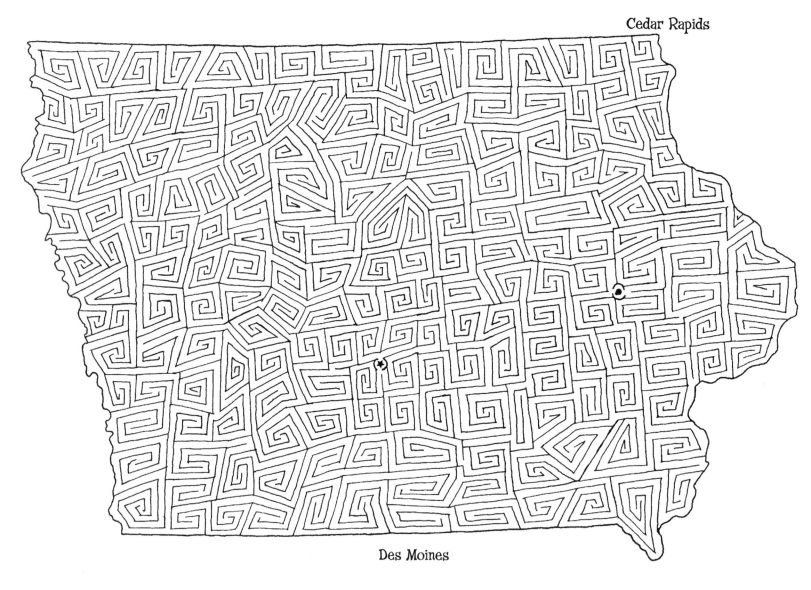

Des Moines

Kansas

Topeka

Wichita

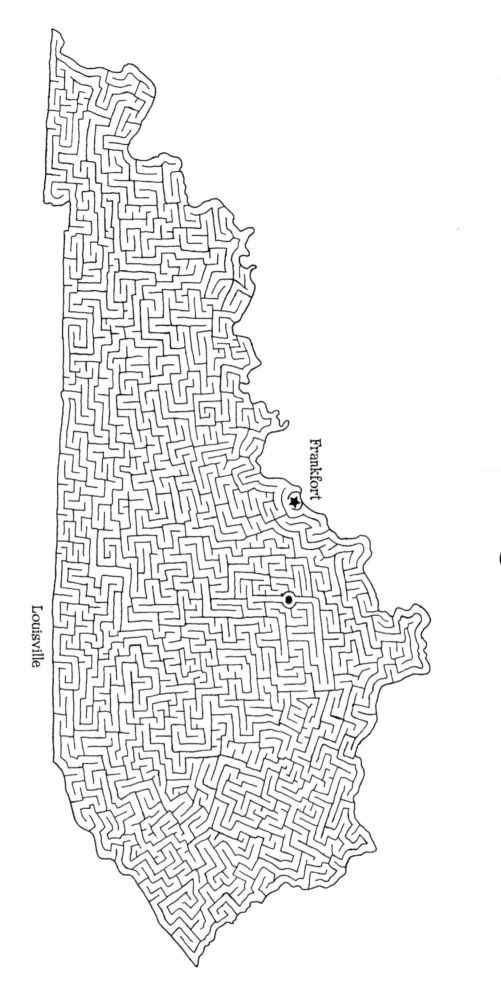

Kentucky

Frankfort

Louisville

Louisiana

Baton Rouge

New Orleans

Maine

Augusta

Portland

Maryland

Baltimore

Annapolis

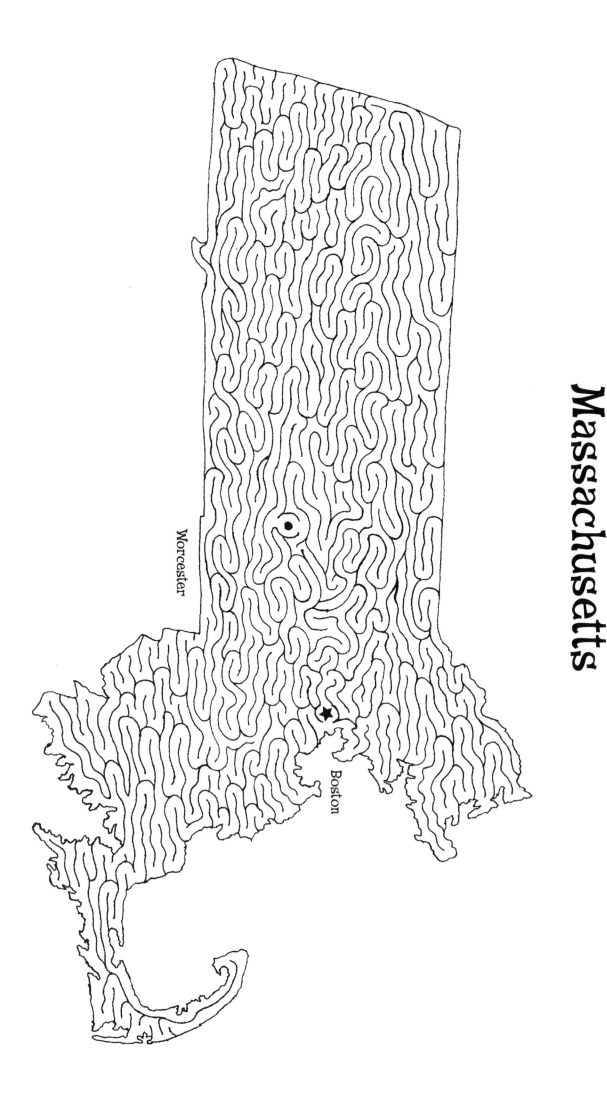

Massachusetts

Worcester

Boston

Michigan

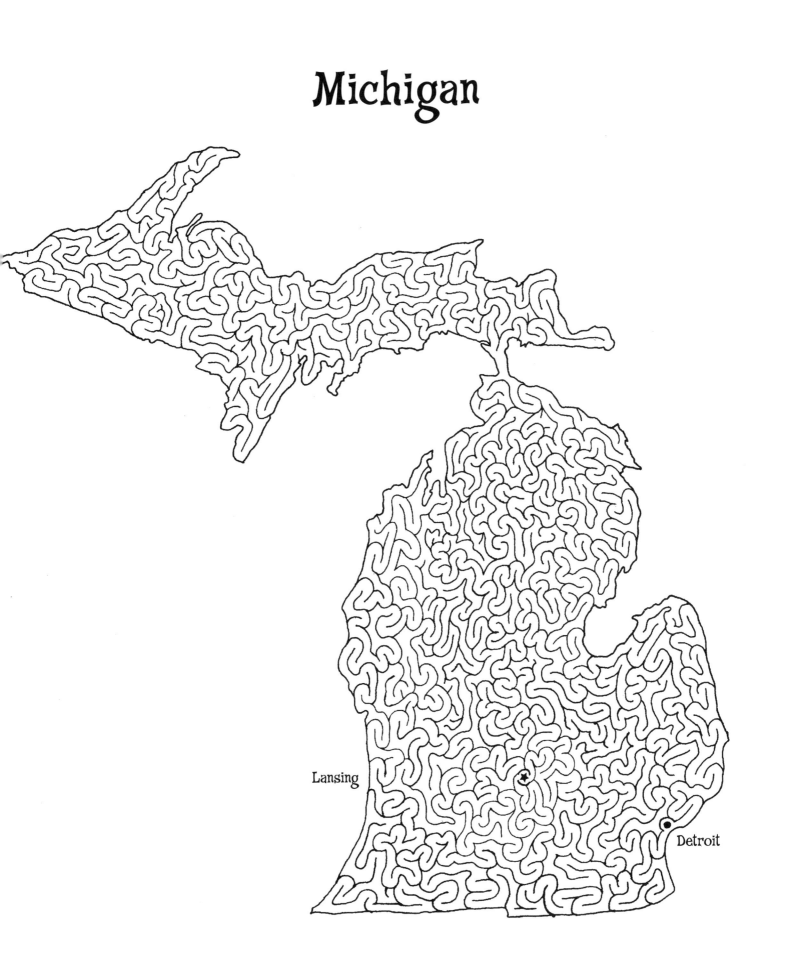

Lansing

Detroit

Minnesota

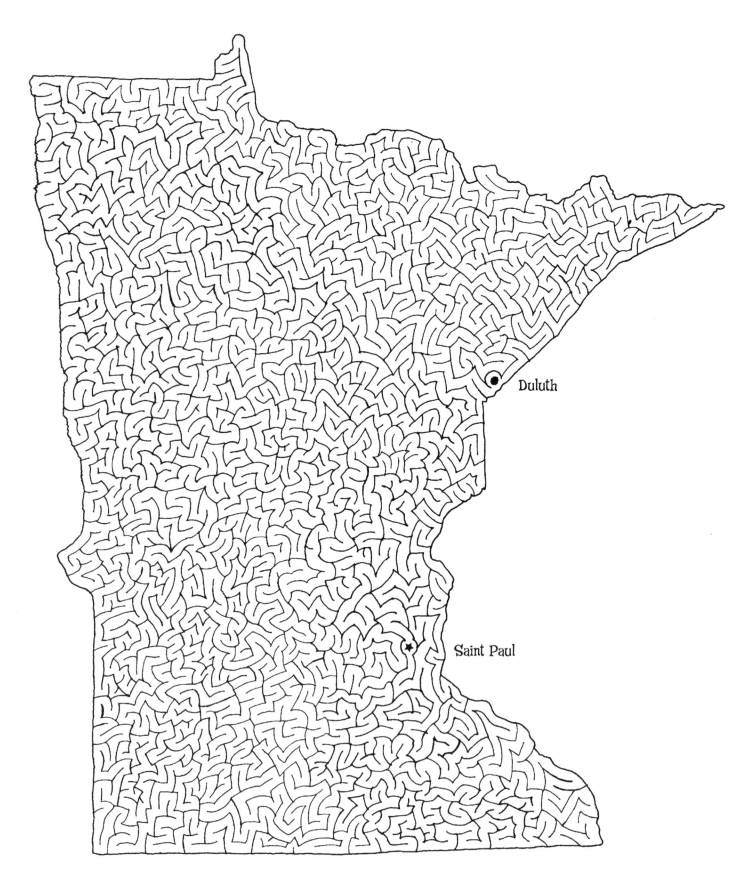

Duluth

Saint Paul

Mississippi

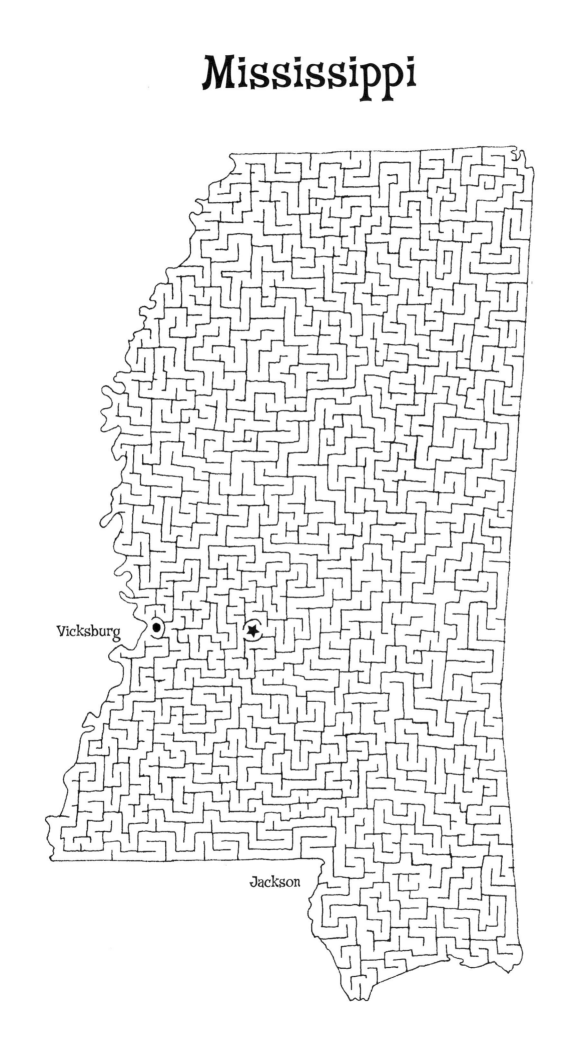

Vicksburg

Jackson

Missouri

St. Louis

Jefferson City

Montana

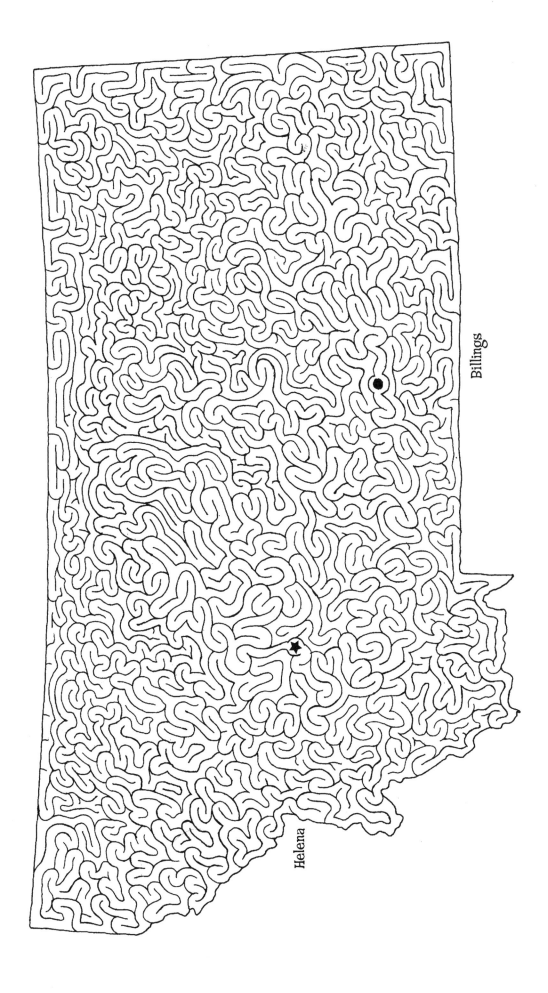

Billings

Helena

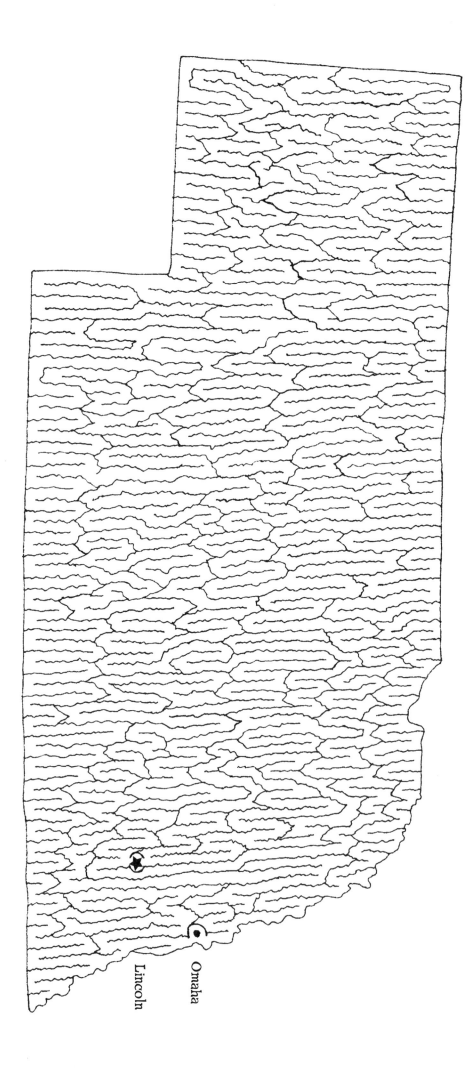

Nebraska

Lincoln

Omaha

Nevada

Carson City

Las Vegas

New Hampshire

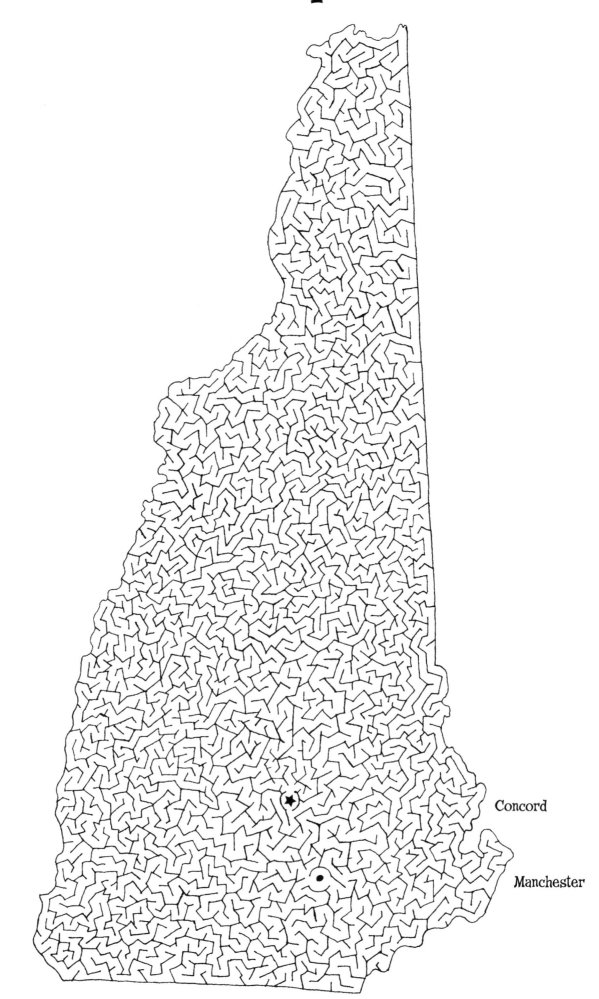

Concord

Manchester

New Jersey

New Mexico

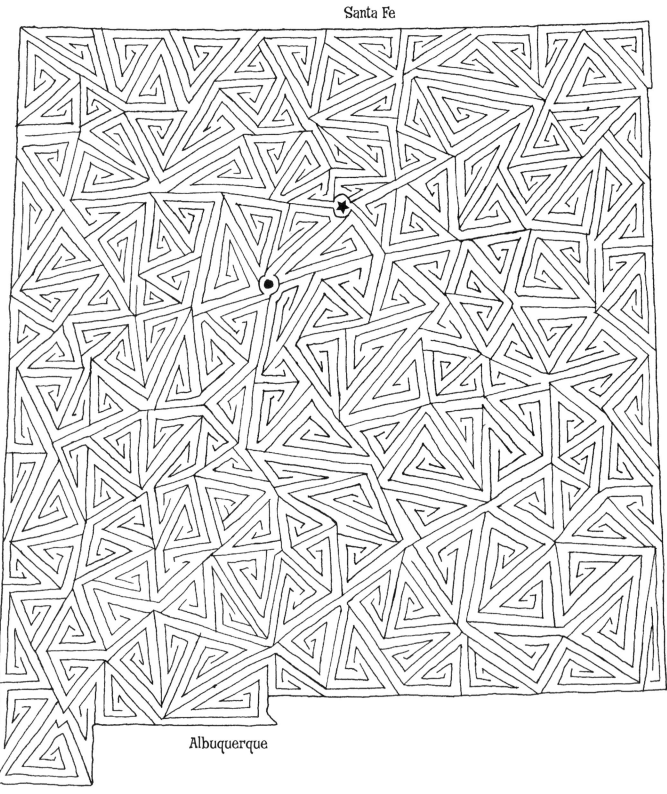

New York

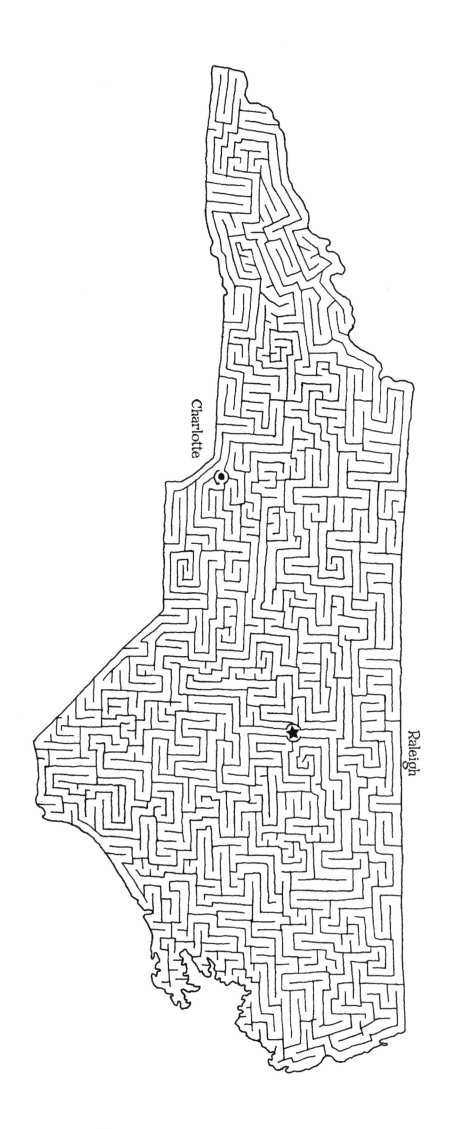

North Carolina

Charlotte

Raleigh

North Dakota

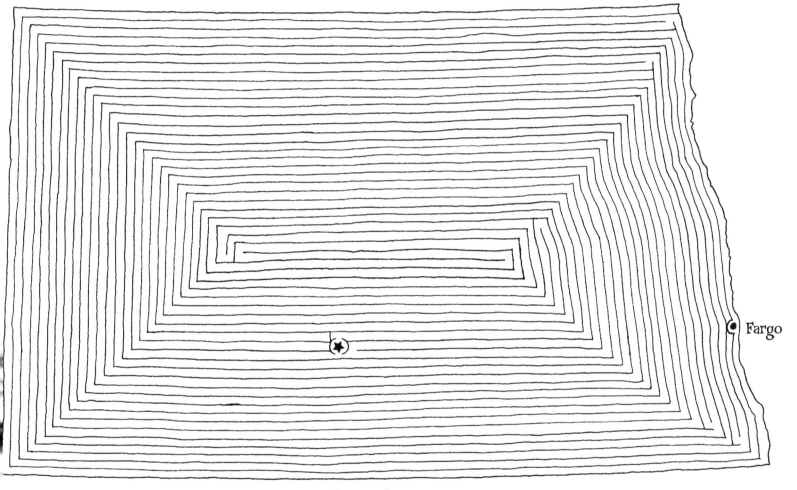

Fargo

Bismarck

Ohio

Oklahoma

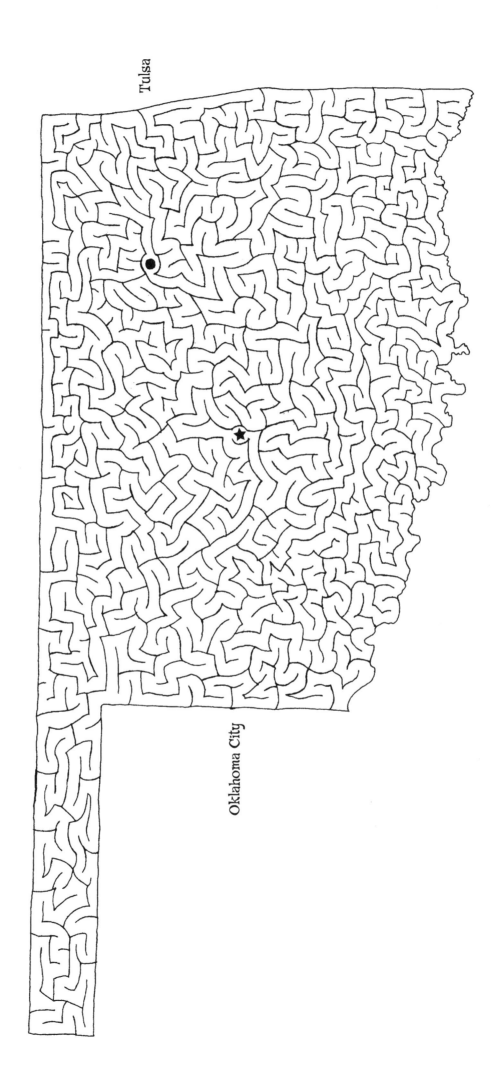

Tulsa

Oklahoma City

Oregon

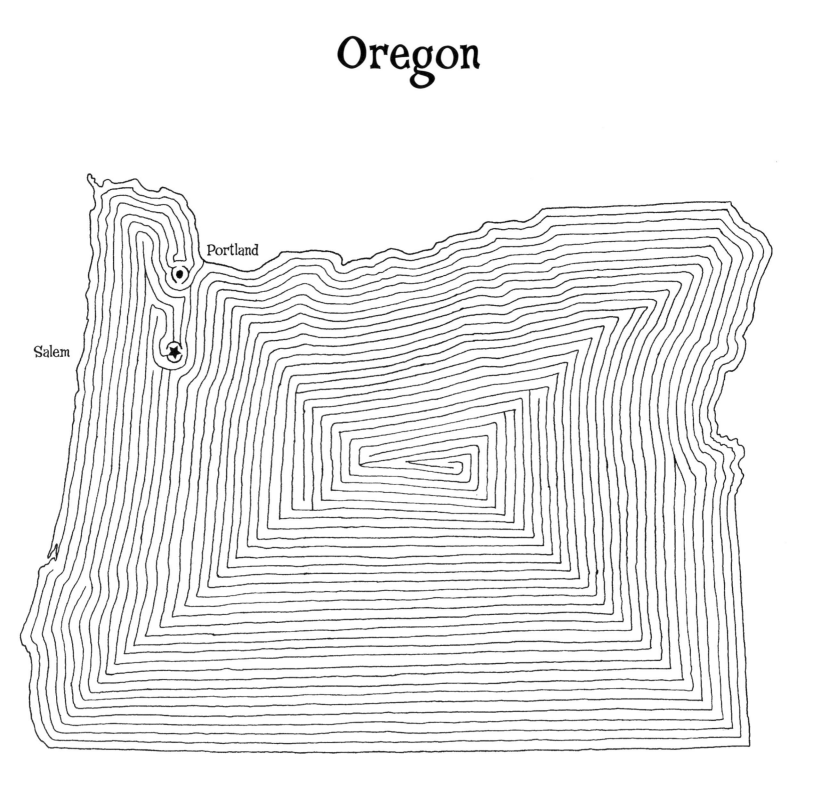

Portland

Salem

Pennsylvania

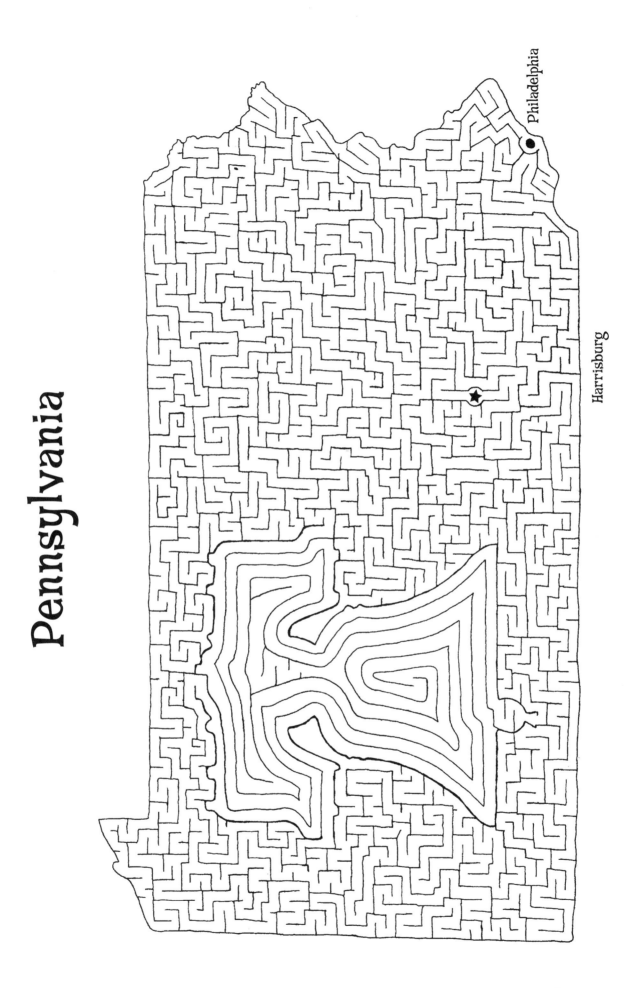

Philadelphia

Harrisburg

Rhode Island

South Carolina

Columbia

Charleston

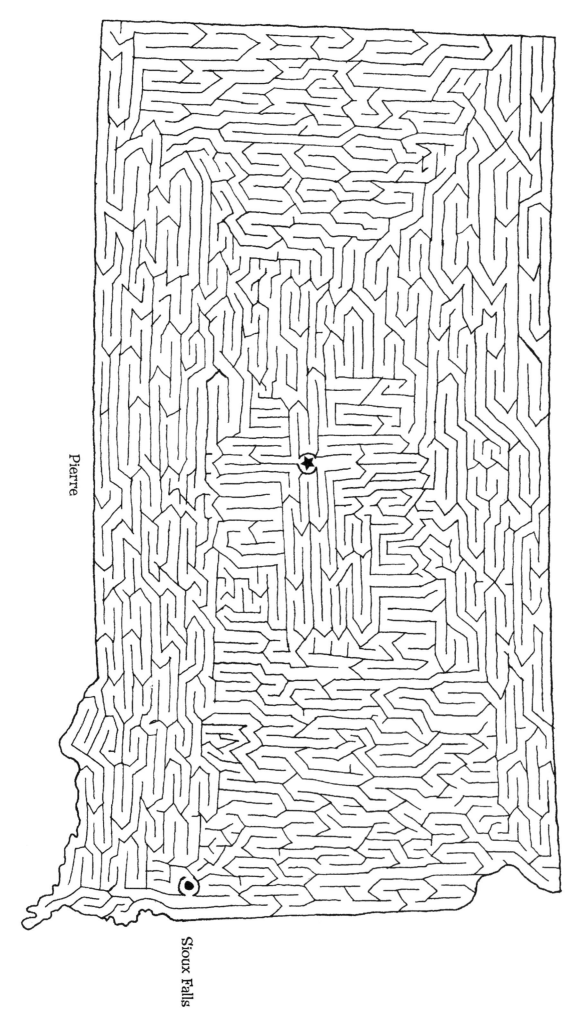

South Dakota

Pierre

Sioux Falls

Tennessee

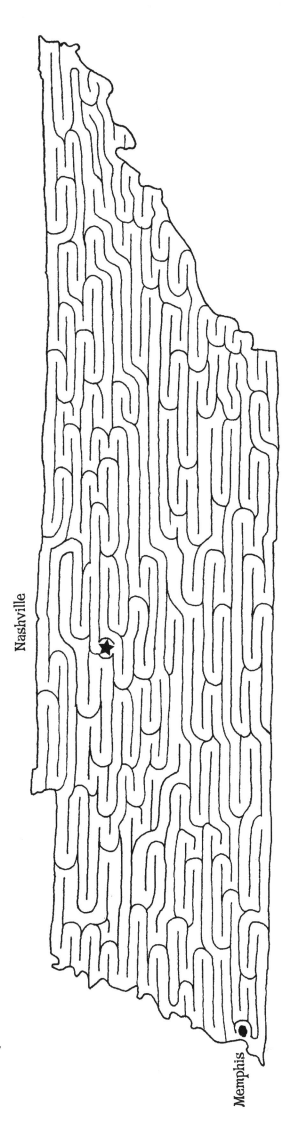

Nashville

Memphis

Texas

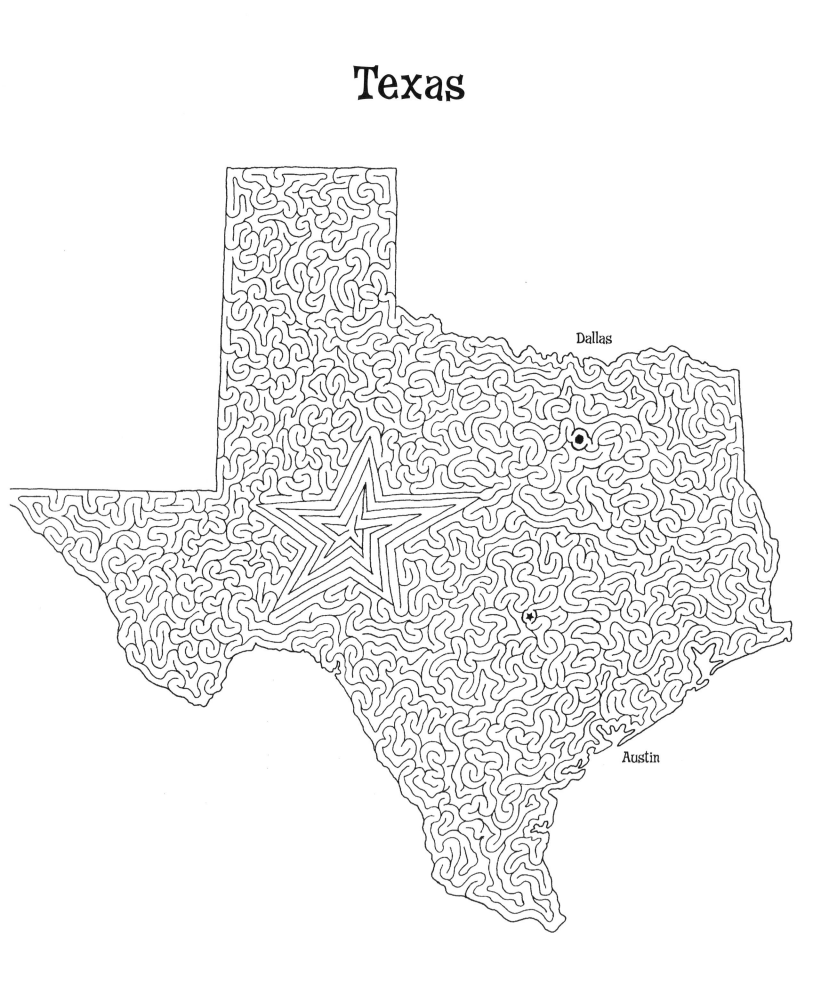

Dallas

Austin

Utah

Salt Lake City

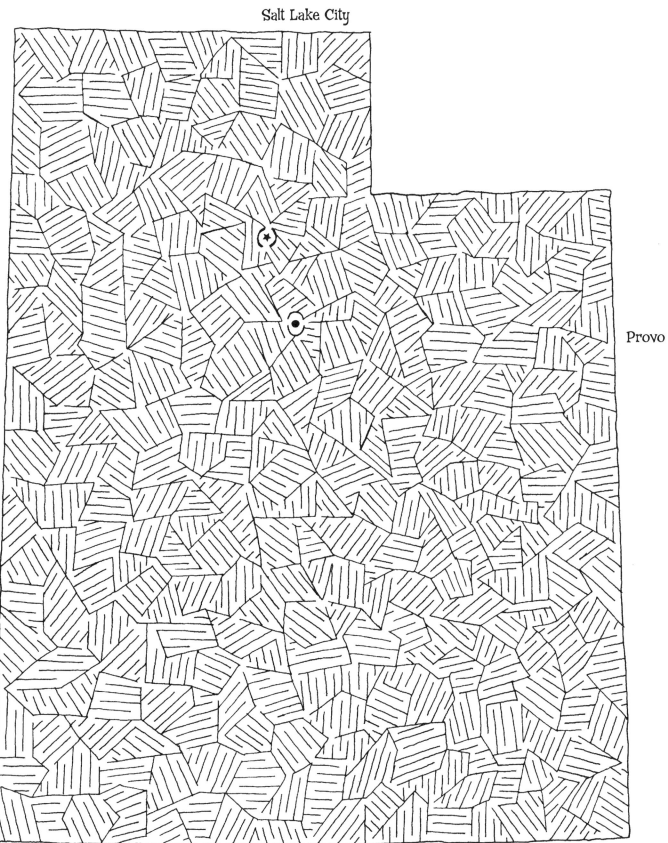

Provo

Vermont

Burlington

Montpelier

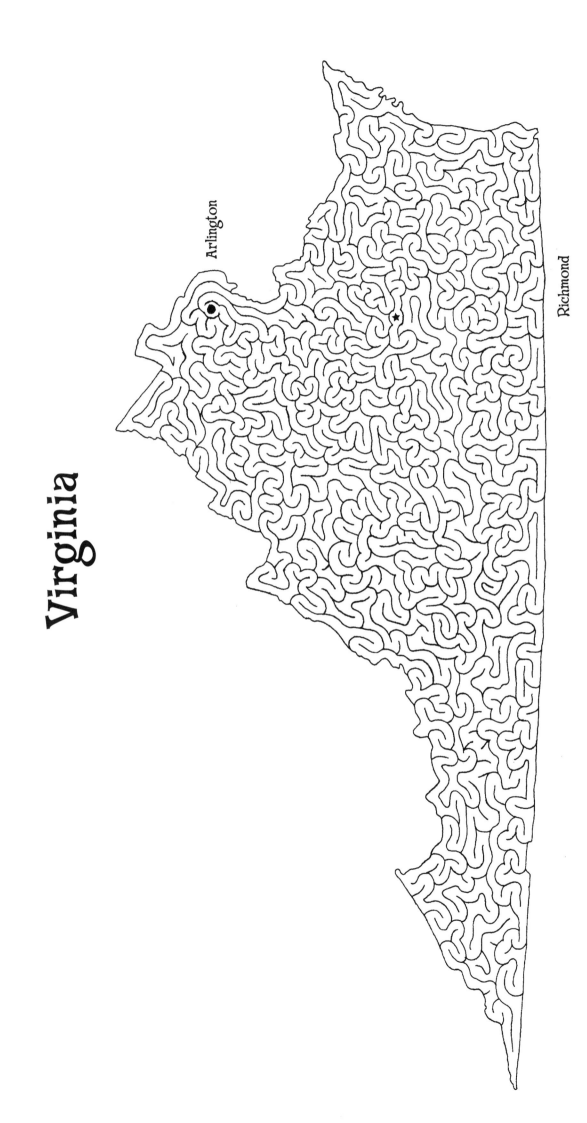

Virginia

Arlington

Richmond

Washington

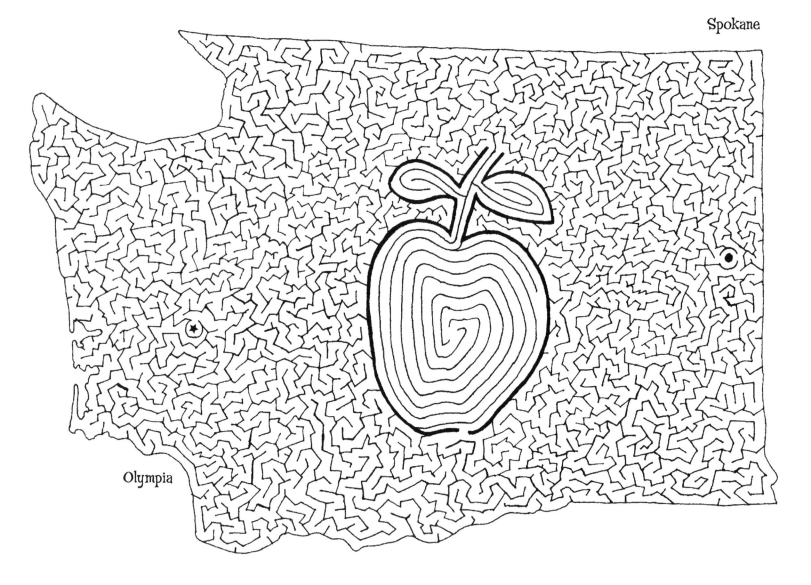

Spokane

Olympia

West Virginia

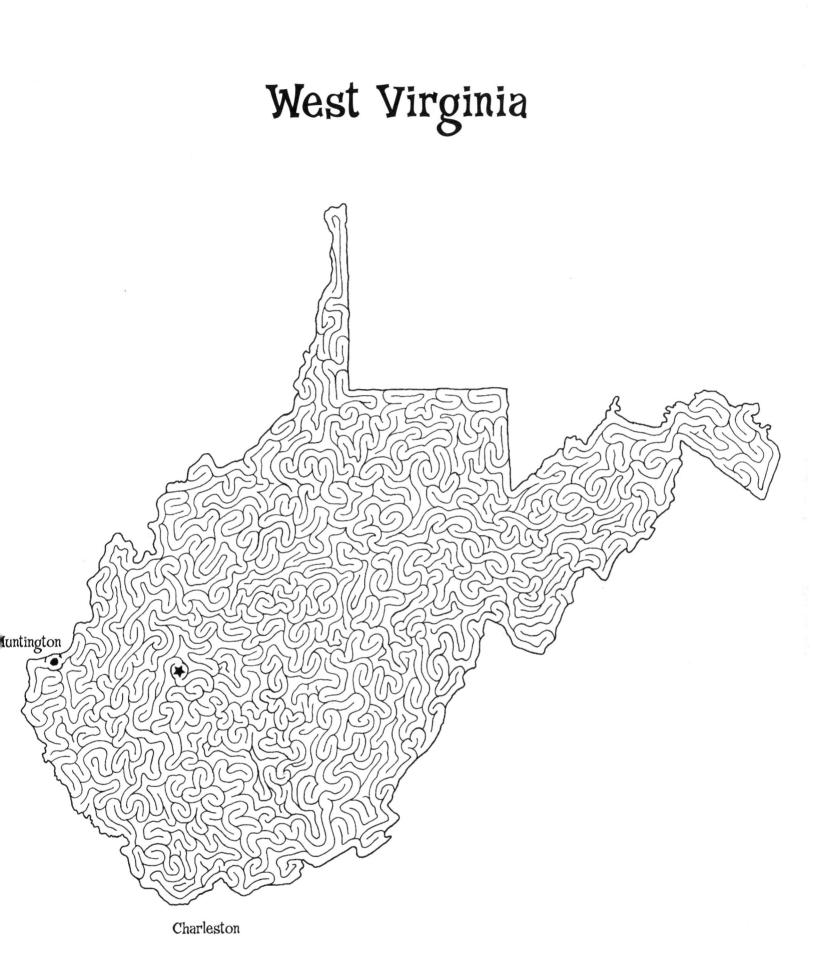

Huntington

Charleston

Wisconsin

Milwaukee

Madison

Wyoming

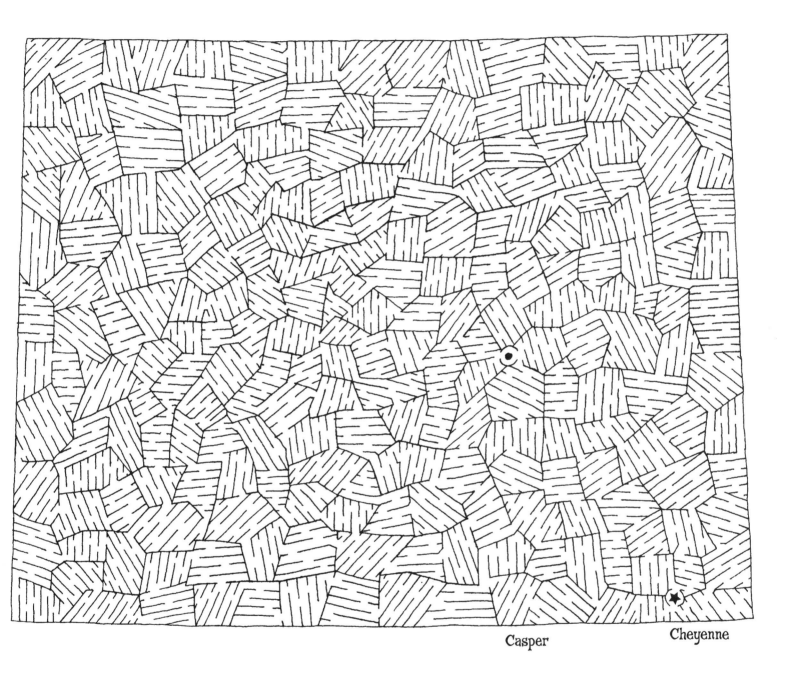

Casper   Cheyenne

★ Solutions ★

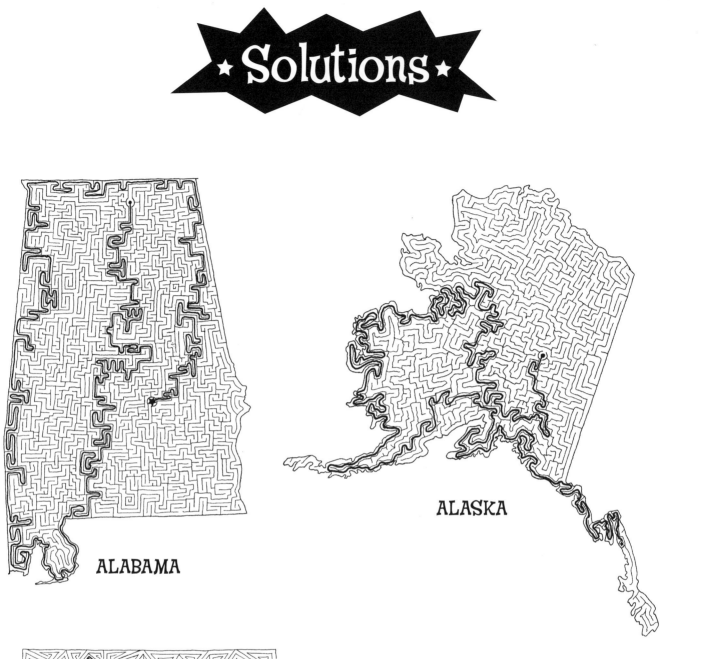

ALABAMA

ALASKA

ARKANSAS

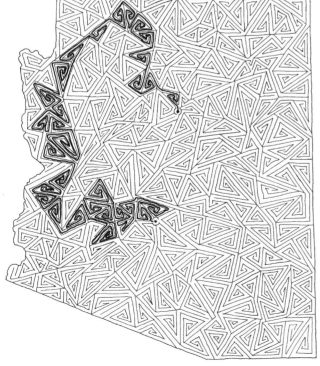

ARIZONA

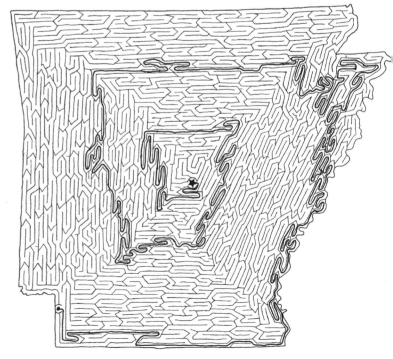

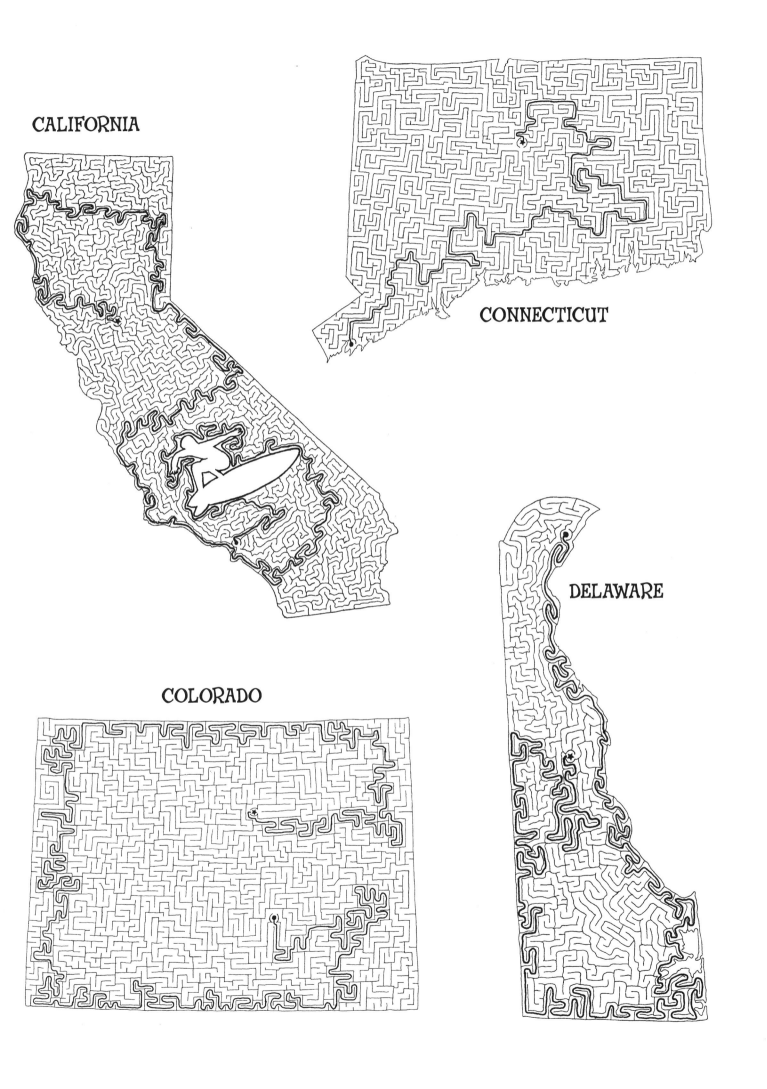

CALIFORNIA

CONNECTICUT

DELAWARE

COLORADO

HAWAII

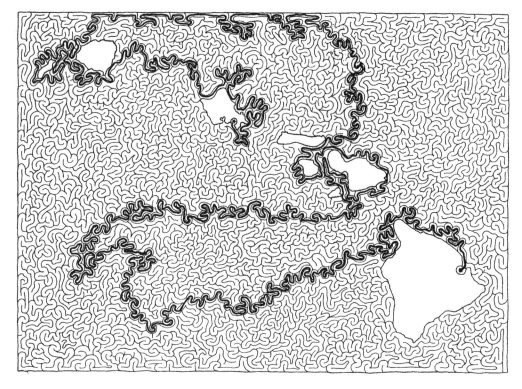

GEORGIA

FLORIDA

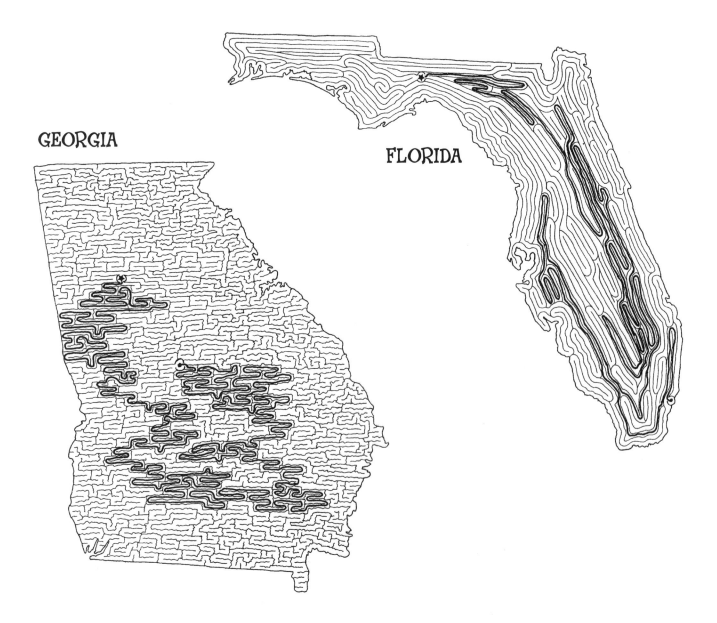

IDAHO

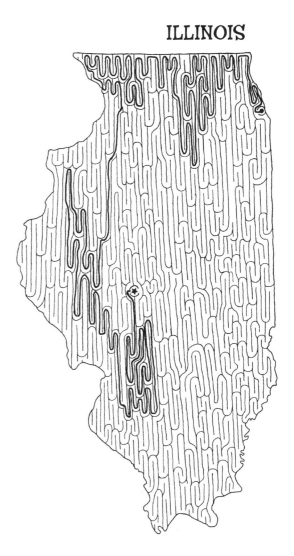

ILLINOIS

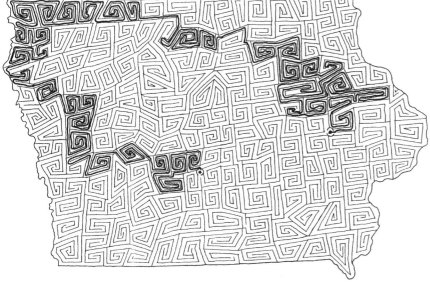

IOWA

INDIANA

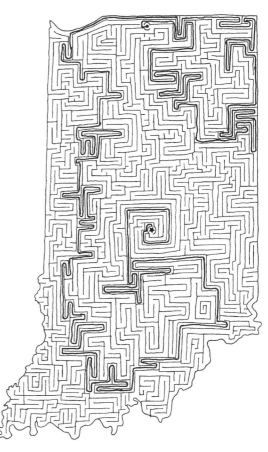

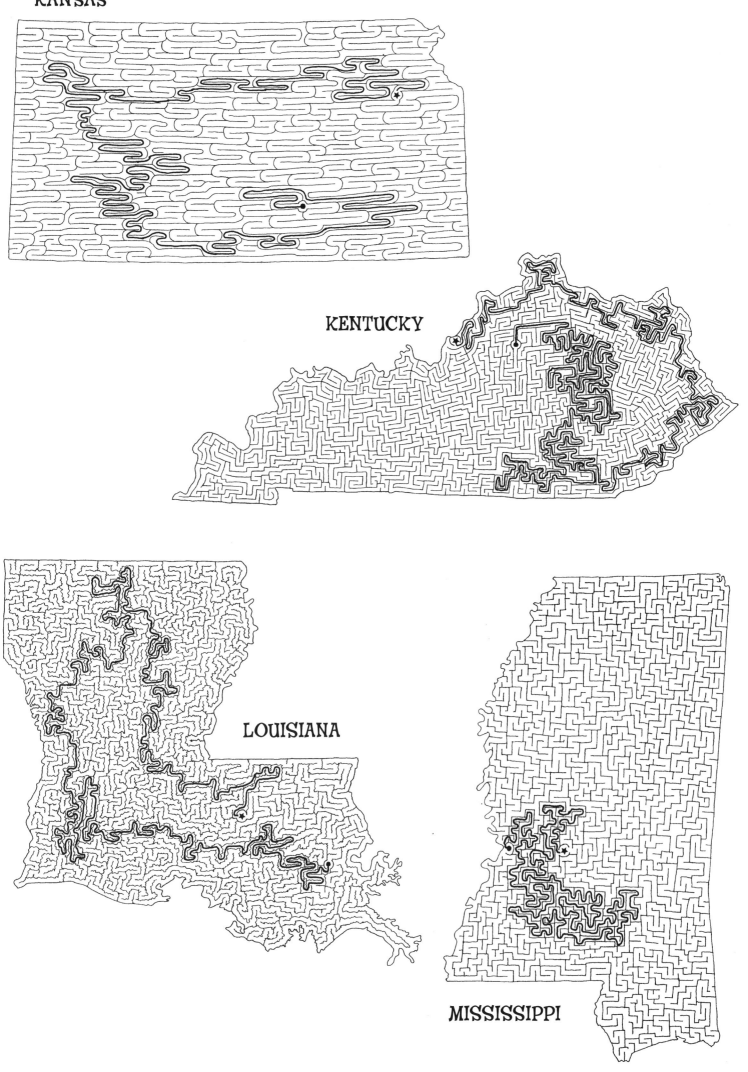

KANSAS

KENTUCKY

LOUISIANA

MISSISSIPPI

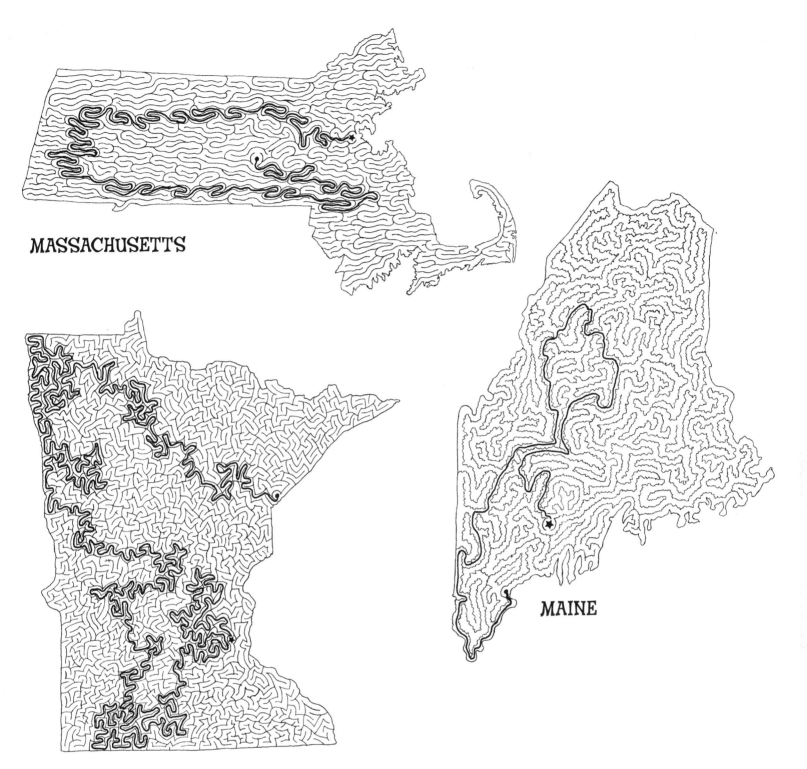

MASSACHUSETTS

MAINE

MINNESOTA

MARYLAND

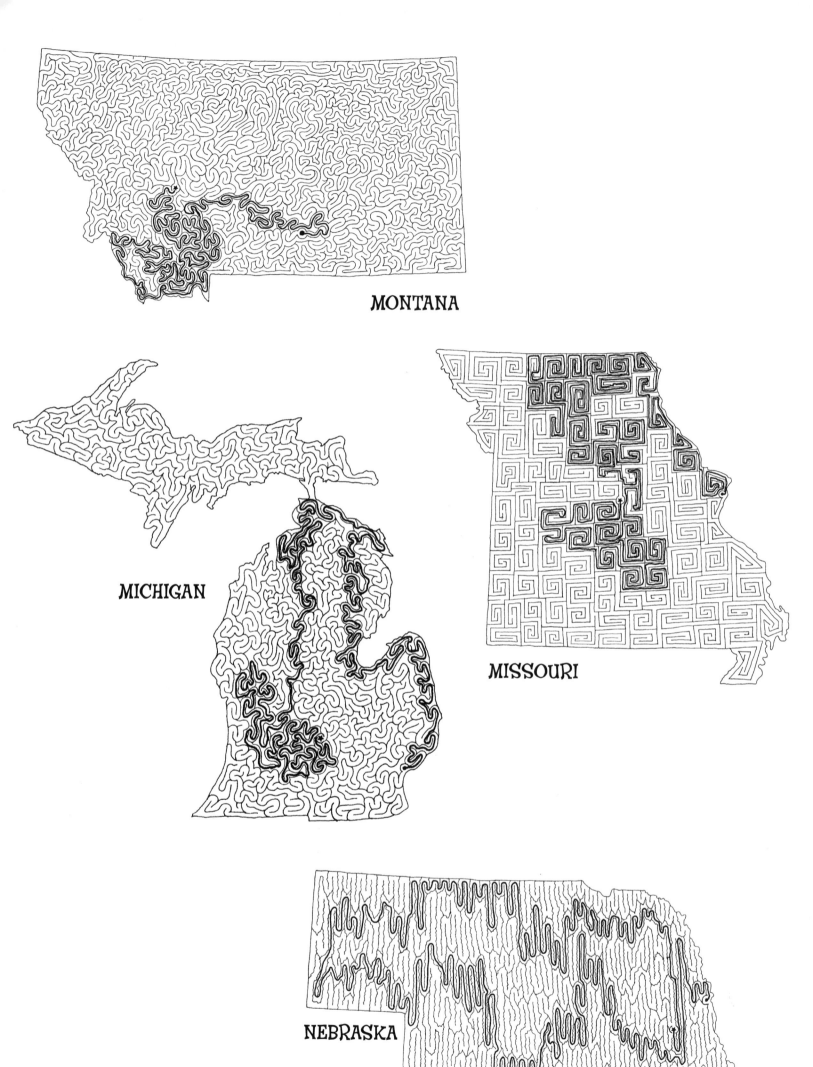

MONTANA

MICHIGAN

MISSOURI

NEBRASKA

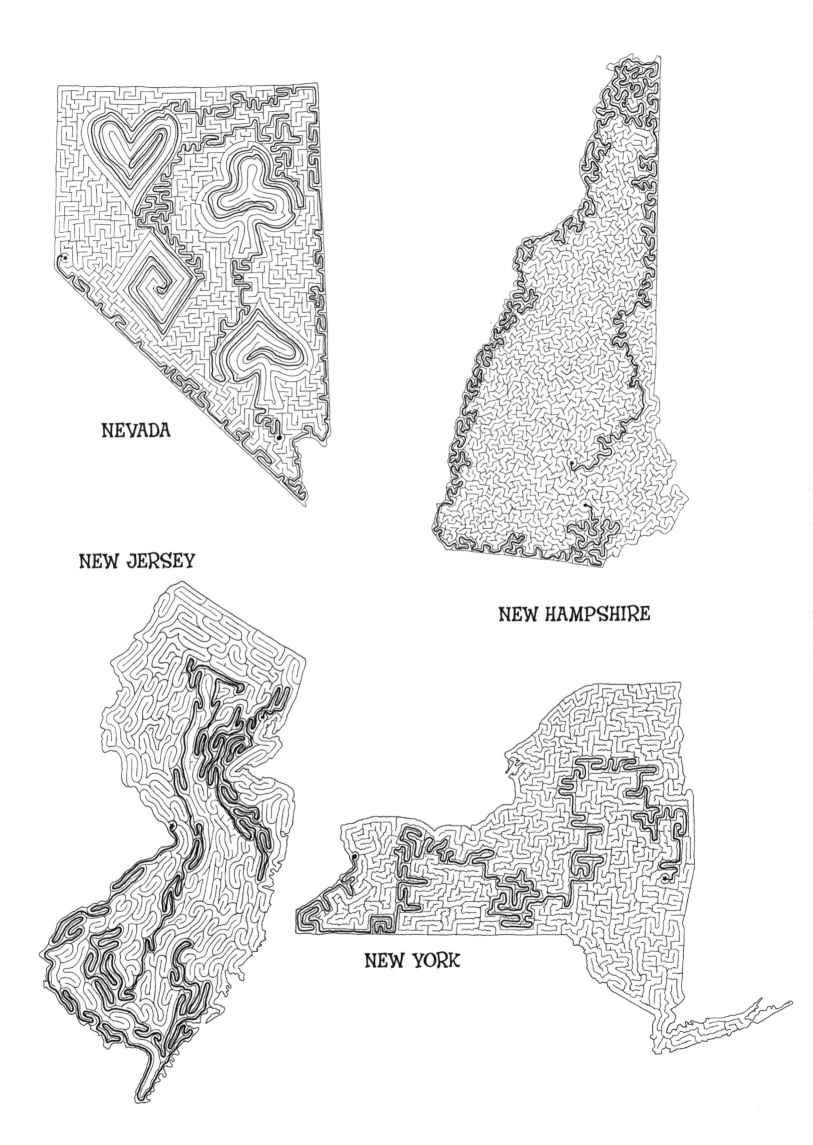

NEVADA

NEW HAMPSHIRE

NEW JERSEY

NEW YORK

NORTH DAKOTA

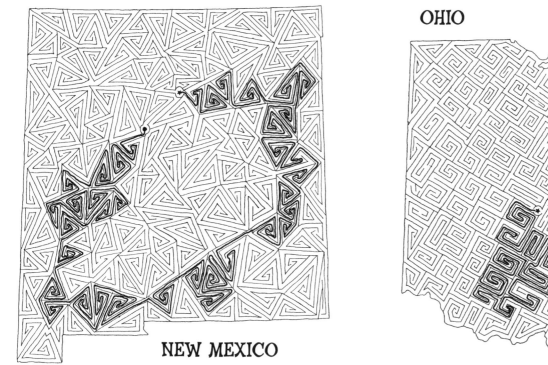

NEW MEXICO

OHIO

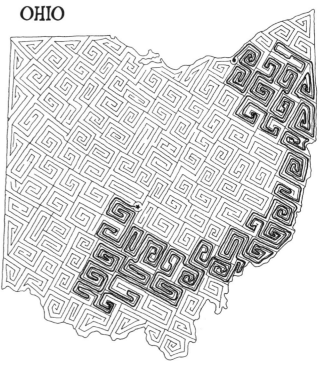

NORTH CAROLINA

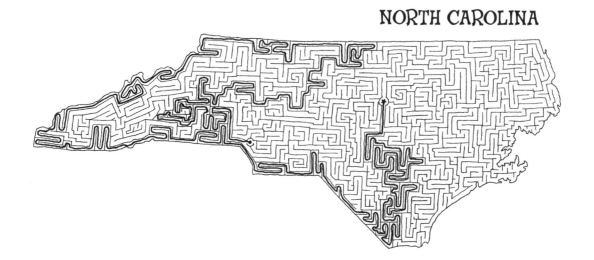

OKLAHOMA

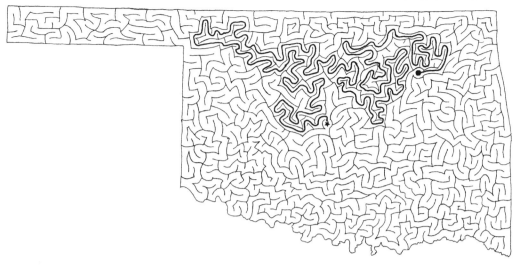

RHODE ISLAND

OREGON

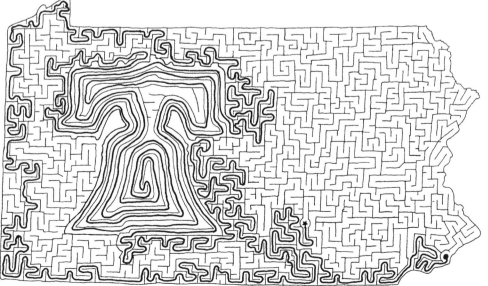

PENNSYVANIA

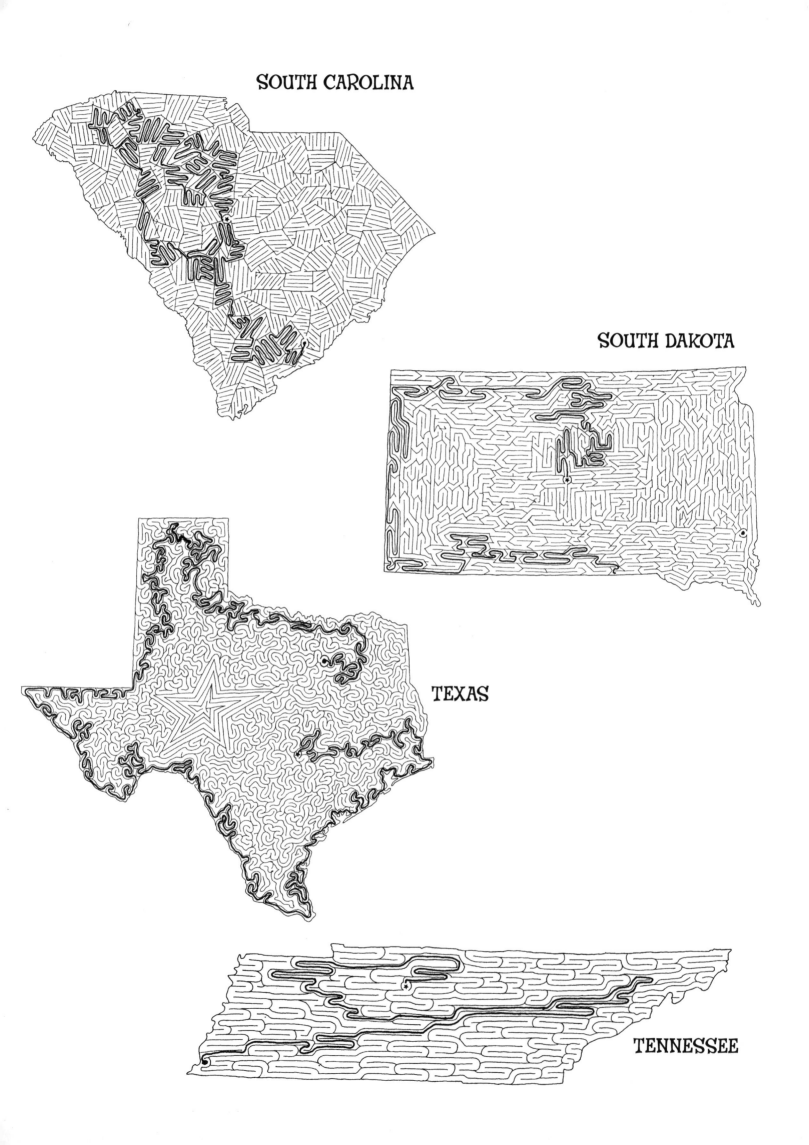

SOUTH CAROLINA

SOUTH DAKOTA

TEXAS

TENNESSEE

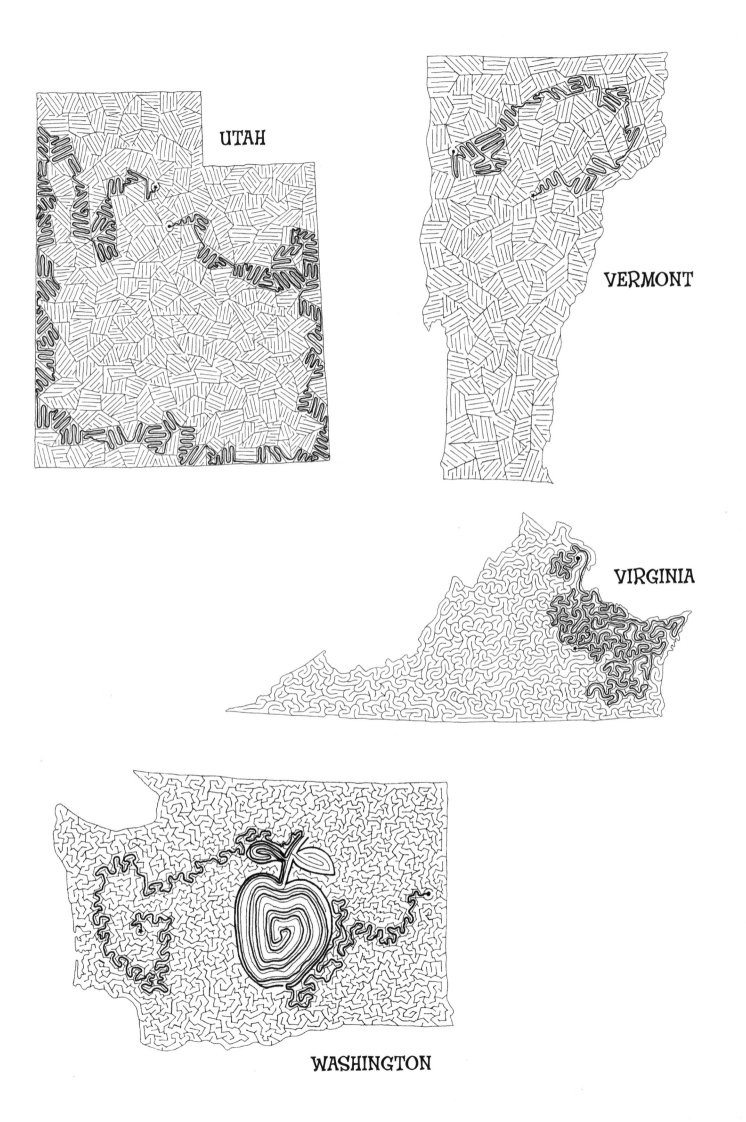

UTAH

VERMONT

VIRGINIA

WASHINGTON

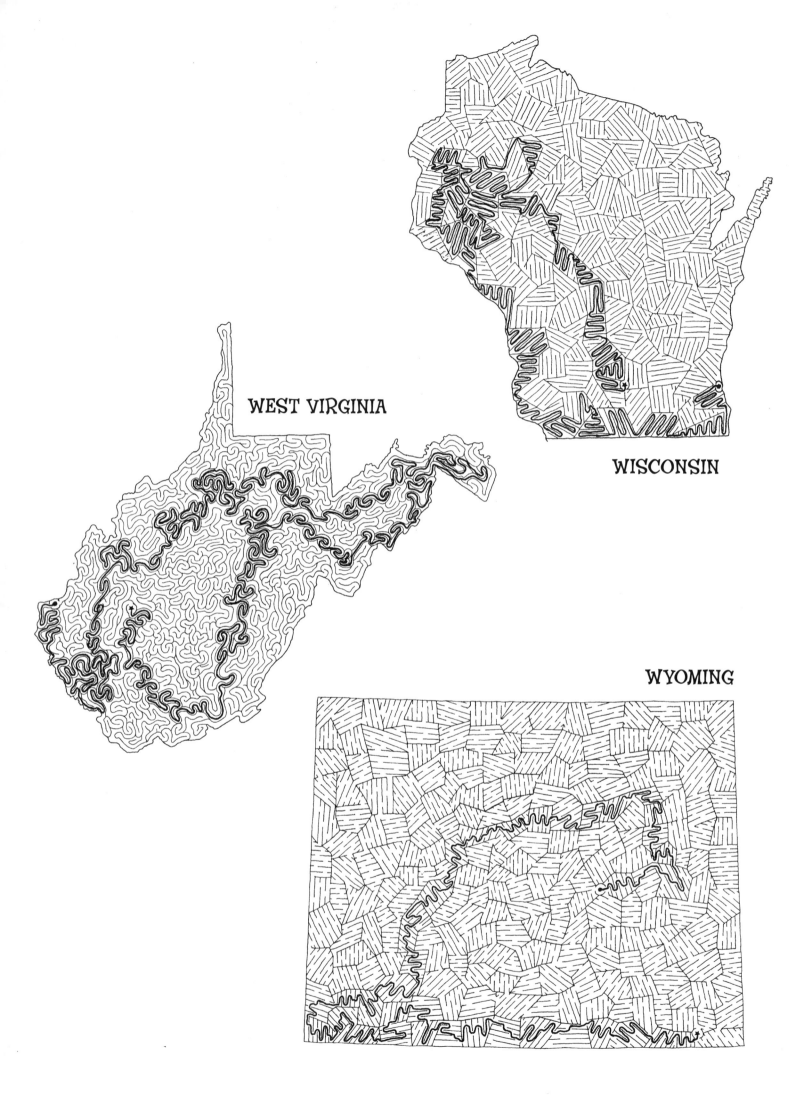

WEST VIRGINIA

WISCONSIN

WYOMING